You Win Some

Some

MIKE WILSON

My luck changed for the better
the day my husband moved out and left me.
I know it sounds daft, but it did.

At first, I thought it was the end of the world.

But then I felt relief.
Relief that I could relax a bit,
and be myself at last.

And then Danny came home
with a wallet he had found.

Someone must have dropped it
just up the road from us,
up by where that nurse lives.

I remember I said to him:

"You're a good boy, Danny,
you've done the right thing.
You've been honest, and I'm proud of you!"

It was the day his father had moved out.

I remember thinking to myself:
it's like a sign, an omen –
better times are on the way!
We're going to be all right!

I said to him:
"Danny, what have you got there?"

He was standing there, looking down,
holding something behind his back.

He held out a man's wallet.
"What shall we do, mum?" he asked.
"Can we keep it?"

I looked in.

Nearly two hundred pounds, there was.
In cash.

There was a business card as well,
a man's name and a phone number.
He worked for that big supermarket – Aztec.

A funny name – Dale Jordan.
He lived out of town somewhere.
What was he doing round here?

I phoned the number,
and told Mr Jordan the good news.
He came round late that evening
to pick the wallet up.

A real smoothie, he was.

I gave him the wallet,
and he opened it and took a look inside.

I said: "Don't worry, love. It's all there!
We haven't taken any!"

"No," he said, "I'm not counting it."
And he took out a twenty pound note.

"It's pretty embarrassing," he went on,
"for a big business man to lose his wallet.
I don't want anyone to know about this."

He held out the twenty pounds.
"Is it a deal?"

I didn't believe his story for one second.
But I said to myself: fair enough.
No questions asked.
Mum's the word!

I spent the money on new trousers for Danny.
He's always wearing out the knees of his trousers.

My next bit of good luck was at work.

The assistant manager's off having a baby,
and they asked me to stand in for her
till she comes back.

Mr Preston said I know you can do it.
I said – I know I can do it as well!
Mr Preston said if I do well and work hard,
I might have a shop of my own one day.

So far it's gone very well,
though I say so myself.

The extra money has come in handy, of course.
But it's not the money.
It's the fact that they had a bit of faith in me.

It's something I've done for myself.
I've built it up from nothing, that job.
And it's given me a lot of confidence in myself.

Just when everything seemed to be falling apart,
everything with Howard and me,
that job showed me
I can be a success at something after all!

And then I met Kenny.

I wasn't looking for a boy-friend.
I mean, Howard had gone,
but I wasn't desperate or anything!
It just sort of happened.

It was just sort of natural.

I met Kenny when he came in the shop,
looking for fabric for curtains, or a duvet cover,
I can't remember what exactly.

The first thing he said to me was:
"You're too good for shop work.
You deserve better."

I said: "But I like it. I like meeting people."
I said: "If I didn't work here,
I wouldn't have met you, would I? "

After that, he came in the shop again and again.

I kept teasing him:
Just how many duvet covers does one man need?

But he just kept coming back for more.

Sometimes I think
what the hell am I doing with this bloke?

Kenny's a DJ.
In a posh disco club down in the town.

And he's ten years younger than me.

We couldn't be more different in lots of ways.

And he's not "Mr Right",
or anything daft like that.

He just cheers me up.
Makes me feel good about myself.
And I need that at the moment.

I remember when he asked me out,
I thought: Oh go on! Give it a go, Val!
Your opinion of men is rock bottom,
it can only go up from here!

So I said yes.

Then again, he is still only twenty nine.
And young for his age.

He looks like a young Neil Diamond.

Maybe that had something to do with it.

So all in all,
things have been quite good lately.

My luck has all been good.
Somewhat surprisingly.

But there's been bad times as well.
I can't forget them.

Seeing Howard.
Fighting.

I can't help it somehow.
Something about him
makes me want to shout at him.
Makes me want to annoy him
and poke fun at him
until I get him to fight back a bit.

He probably never will, though.

One of life's little losers,
that's our Howard.

And then there's Danny
It's not exactly a bed of roses
with little Danny these days.

Sometimes he's out till nearly midnight.
I have no idea where he goes, or who he's with.

Sometimes he goes very quiet,
and lost inside himself.

I look at him,
and it's like he's the lodger, or something.
He's this stranger I share my house with,
who reminds me of the son I used to have...

I've no idea what he thinks of Kenny.

Kenny tries really hard with him,
takes him out, buys him things...

Once in a while, I let Kenny stay the night,
and I really make a fuss of Danny the next day,
just so he won't feel left out...

But he just goes quiet and small, all the time,
so you can't tell what he's thinking or feeling,
and I can't get near him.

He needs a man about the place.

And now this.

I don't know what to make of this.

I'm not sure if this is more good luck,
or more trouble than it's worth!

This is how it all started.
June came in to work one day
with a magazine about holidays.
It was called Away!

I had a look at it at coffee time.
There was a competition to win a free holiday –
two-weeks in a hotel in the Caribbean.

I could just do with that, I thought.

So I had a look at what you had to do.
I was surprised –
I could answer some of the questions.

What is the capital of Jamaica? Easy.
Which is bigger, Trinidad or Tobago? Easy.
Name five of the Windward Islands...

Well, some questions were a bit hard,
but I could look up the answers easy enough.

The big problem was going to be the caption.
You know, the bit where it says:

Complete this sentence in less than 12 words:
I deserve a 14-day Caribbean Hotel Holiday
with Away! magazine because...

That's the killer.
What would I put?

I thought of so many – all no good:

I deserve a Caribbean Hotel Holiday, because
my husband Howard just walked out on me
and left me to look after our nine year old son
all on my own.

No. I don't think so.
Anyway, it's slightly more than twelve words.

I deserve a Caribbean Hotel Holiday, because
I have never been on a holiday abroad
except The Channel Islands.

Pathetic.

I deserve a Caribbean Hotel Holiday, because
I'll work all my life,
and never afford one any other way.

True, maybe. But not likely to win.

In the end I just made up a load of old rubbish,
I couldn't think of anything else.

My twelve words were:

1	Work	7	Breathe
2	Family	8	Rest
3	Stress	9	Relax
4	Sun	10	Rum
5	Sea	11	And
6	Beach	12	Coke.

Oh well, I thought to myself,
I've had a run of good luck so far.
It had to change sooner or later!

Then I posted the whole lot off
to Away! magazine,
and forgot all about it.

Believe it or not, I don't scream a lot at work.
It's not the way we like to do things at Fenway's.

For one thing:
let's face it – it's not all that exciting,
selling curtain fabrics and bed linen.

And we don't often get visits from Richard Gere.

And I'm not scared of mice.

So all in all I don't do much screaming at work.

But I did scream once.

I'll never forget that day.

Just after nine one morning,
Mr Preston came over to me
and said I was wanted on the phone.

Oh no, I was thinking.
I hope it's not Danny's school...

I took the call in Mr Preston's office,
while he waited out in the shop.

"Is that Mrs Davenport?" said a man's voice.

I said it was.

"I'm sorry to trouble you at work," he went on,
"but I'm phoning from Away! magazine.
"It's my pleasant duty to inform you
that you are the lucky winner of our..."

It was then that I screamed at work.
Right there in Mr Preston's office.

Mr Preston peeped round the door.
He looked quite frightened.
"Is everything all right, Val?" he hissed.
"Not bad news I hope?"

The man from the magazine was saying:
"...really liked your caption for the competition
...very different and original...and er...
Mrs Davenport?
Are you still there, Mrs Davenport?"

I couldn't speak.
I couldn't breathe.
All I could do was stand there,
thinking about Caribbean sunshine,
and looking at Mr Preston.

I'd never noticed until that moment
just how old and shabby Mr Preston was.

The letter came through a few days later.

By then, everyone in the street knew.

Jackie Warner had been round,
with half a bottle of bubbly to celebrate!

Her husband Stan told me
if I needed a butler on the holiday,
he'd come along and give me a hand!

Stan said it was better than winning The Lottery,
because there was skill in what I had done.
It wasn't just the luck of the draw!

Then Mr Hussain said "Well done" to me
one day when I popped into his shop,
and Mrs Hussain gave me some lovely flowers!

Everyone's been so nice...

Even that new couple, the Dempseys,
called "Congratulations!" over the road to me!
They seem very nice...

But.

There was a problem.

It had to happen some time, didn't it?

The problem was:

When the letter came from Away! magazine,
it said two people.

I had won a two-week holiday in the Caribbean
for two people.

And I didn't know what to do,
because I didn't know who to take with me.

If I went with Kenny,
Danny could stay with his father.
It might be good for him to see his dad. . .

But what would Danny think of me
if I went on a holiday without him?

And what would Howard get up to
while I was out of the way?
He'd try to turn my little Danny against me.

We're growing apart as it is.
Things might never be the same between us
if Danny spent a fortnight with his father.
I'd lose him. I know I would.

No. Better to take Danny with me.
Kenny will understand.

But then I started thinking:
What if Kenny doesn't understand?

How is he going to feel?

He's the best thing to happen to me in years,
and I can't just brush him to one side,
and go off enjoying myself without him.

Would he still be waiting for me when I got back?

I'm too old to risk losing him.
I may not get a chance like this again.

I may not get my hands on anyone like him again!

And it would be so wonderful with Kenny there!
We'd be sailing off into beautiful sun-sets,
hand in hand, arm in arm,
in the warm romantic Caribbean evenings!

What would I do if I took Danny with me?

Pack him off for an early night (for a change)
so I can curl up in my own bed
with a good Mills and Boon?

I can't see it somehow.
It's got to be Kenny.

But then – what will happen to Danny?

It went on like this for weeks.
I just couldn't make up my mind.

I talked it over again and again
with Jackie Warner and with my Mum,
and with Dee from next door.
But I got no nearer to an answer.

Danny wouldn't talk about it.
And Kenny was saying nothing.
He was just waiting to see what would happen.

Everyone was watching me,
waiting to see what would happen!

I was lying awake at night,
trying to make sense of it all,
and going to work with bags under my eyes.
It was worse than all that mess with Howard!

But I couldn't make my mind up.

One way or the other,
someone was going to lose out.
Someone was going to get hurt.

In the end, I got another phone call at work.
It was the man from Away! magazine.
He needed to know what was going on.
He was running out of time.

"If you don't tell me here and now," he said,
"you can wave goodbye to the Caribbean!
Because you'll never see it!"

All of a sudden, I knew what I had to do.

"All right," I said to him.
"I'll fill in the form tonight.
You'll get it in the post by Friday."

And I told him who was going,
so he could make the booking.

Then I walked out of Mr Preston's office
and went straight in to the Ladies
and had a bit of a cry.

But afterwards, I felt much better.
I just dried my eyes and blew my nose
and went and got on with my work.

I knew I had done the right thing.

They set off this morning.

I saw them off in the taxi.

They wanted me to go with them
all the way to the airport,
and wave them off from there.

But I said no, it's all right.
I'll stay here.

Of course, they didn't want to go at first.
Everyone said it was my holiday,
I won it and I must not give it away.

But women are always making a sacrifice,
aren't they?
To sons and husbands and lovers.
Making a sacrifice.
Keeping everybody happy.
It's what women do best.

My mum and dad won't get another holiday.
They can't afford it. Not now he's retired.
So I gave in their names to Away! magazine.

It was mum and dad who flew off this morning
for the holiday of a lifetime.

It was my thank you to them.

In the end, it's all worked out pretty well.

Danny's quite happy about everything.

He's just got a place in the school football team.
He didn't want to go away and miss a match
in case he lost his place!

He didn't even want to go
on a Caribbean Hotel Holiday!

Kenny's not too happy of course.

He lost his temper a bit.
He said a few things.
Things he didn't mean.

He stormed out, but he'll be back.
He'll sulk a bit, but he'll get over it.
I know he will.

I said to myself – there's more to life than this!
All this worry over a two week holiday, when
we've got the rest of our lives to look forward to!

No. I'm not worried.
It's not the end of the world.

I'm stronger now.
And if Kenny really loves me,
he'll be back.